Behold the Lamb of God
Communion Prayers for the Sick

Written & compiled by
Penny Hickey, OCDS

Witness Ministries
825 S. Waukegan Rd., A8-200
Lake Forest, Illinois 60045
847-735-0556/800-484-5350, code 5255

Scripture texts are taken from the *New American Bible* © 1970 Confraternity of Christian Doctrine, 3211 Fourth St., N.E., Washington, D.C. 20017-1194, and are used by license of the copyright owner. All rights reserved. No part of the *New American Bible* may be reproduced in any form without the permission of the copyright holder.

The texts in this book may not be used in place of the official liturgical texts found in *Pastoral Care of the Sick*.

All quotes from Carmelite Saints and Blesseds used with kind permission.

Light Love Life. Edited by Conrad De Meester, OCD, and the Carmel of Dijon. Translated by Sr. Aletheia Kane, OCD. © 1987.
Self Portrait in Letters. Translated by Josephine Koeppel, OCD. © 1993.
Story of a Soul. Translated by John Clarke, OCD. © 1975, 1976.
The Collected Works of St. Teresa of Avila, Vol. II. Translated by Kieran Kavanaugh, OCD, and Otilio Rodriguez, OCD. © 1980.
All rights reserved by The Washington Province of Discalced Carmelites, Inc. ICS Publications, 2131 Lincoln Road, N.E., Washington, D.C. 20002 U.S.A.

Love in the Heart of the Church. Christopher O'Donnell, O.CARM. © 1997. First published by Veritas Publications. Used with permission.

ISBN: 0-9640417-6-6

Foreword

There is a new Pentecost, a heightening of religious awareness in our world today. Whether it is due to the saturation broadcasting of religious programs on our electronic media, or the increases in literacy and the availability of Bibles in almost any language, it is difficult to say without an extensive survey. Another avenue is also open: the finding of God in times of illness. We are perhaps more aware of severe illness, the millions spent on research and the close coverage of all hints of a cure.

There is a need for a few good prayerbooks for times of serious illness. Many times the person finds it very difficult to pray. All of their person seems to be focused and harnessed to just coping with the illness. Some pastoral ministers, with an abundance of good will, may visit and also find it difficult to pray an appropriate prayer.

Behold the Lamb of God by Penny Hickey was written to directly come to the aid of the pastoral minister, and indirectly to come to the aid of the persons suffering and experiencing a prayer block. I searched many religious book shelves during my eight years of hospital ministry. Hopefully this handy little book of prayers will introduce some pastoral persons and patients to some new ways of praying during illness.

The reflections and prayers in *Behold the Lamb of God* are taken from many Carmelite authors. The original Carmelites come from the Wadi e'Siah, the Valley of the Hermits, near the fountain of Elijah, in the southwest part of Haifa in Israel. The hermits there had ministered to pilgrims on their way to pray at the holy places. In a recent archaeological dig, a shrub was found amongst the ruins that yielded a medicinal herb.

The Carmelites in the United States now include about 7500 lay members, such as Penny Hickey, working in retirement homes, hospitals and private homes. They also include about one thousand contemplative nuns, three thousand active sisters, two hundred friars and a few hermits.

The format of the prayers also facilitates the distribution of the Eucharist to the sick and hurting.

Hopefully, the reflections and prayers, gleaned from some of the Carmelites of the last few hundred years, will still continue to heal the body and soul of our people.

Fr. Theodore N. Centala, OCD
OCDS Provincial Delegate

Author's Preface

J esus in the Blessed Sacrament is the Divine Physician and Remedy of the sick and suffering. As Jesus walked the earth He healed all those who came to Him. At Lourdes many of the miracles of healing occur with the blessing of Jesus in the monstrance. How blessed we are to have Him available daily in Holy Communion! The moment of receiving Him is the most intimate encounter and heart to heart exchange between God and man.

This booklet is written to assist those who carry Communion to the sick and shut-ins. There are some who find it difficult to pray spontaneously. Perhaps these offerings will encourage them. The little book was composed after a specific request for such a work. Suffering is a part of life for each of us. It may be physical, mental or moral affliction. Since we are integrated beings, we are often affected in more than one area at a given time. These prayers therefore are also suitable meditations for anyone who has been invited to share in the Cross.

Each section includes a relevant Scripture quote, a spontaneous prayer suggestion and a quote from a Saint or Blessed. More than one of these prayer suggestions could be combined. The Scriptures and quotes of the Saints are interchangeable as well. Jesus loves each of us uniquely, by name. He never touches us generally or "generically." That is why each prayer includes the prompt [name]. The spontaneous prayers are worded simply, as cries to compassionate Jesus for help.

There are several reasons for using the quotes from these particular Saints and Blesseds. I am a Secular Discalced Carmelite and am most familiar with them. The Saints suffered greatly while on earth; they were no strangers to pain. Most of the Saints lived in modern times. St. Teresa of the Andes was born in 1900 and died in 1920. Bl. Mary of Jesus Crucified (the Little Arab) was born in 1846 and died in 1878. St. Therese of Lisieux was born in 1873 and died in 1897. Bl. Elizabeth of the Trinity was born in 1880 and died in 1906. Bl. Bakanja Isidore died in 1909. St. Teresa Benedicta of the Cross (Edith Stein) died in 1942 in Auschwitz, and Bl. Titus Brandsma was martyred at Dachau in the same year. Fr. Jacques Bunel died in 1945 from injuries by the Nazis. Their quotes reflect a peace and joy in suffering that only God can give. As He has given to them, He continues to give to all who call upon Him.

My husband John and I reside in Pennsylvania where John retired after thirty years in the Army. We have been blessed with four children: Rosemary, John III, Mike and Jeff. I have been a Eucharistic Minister to the sick for fourteen years, serving in homes, hospitals and a retirement home. I am a registered nurse, although not currently employed. Having had numerous knee operations, and spending almost sixteen years on crutches with much time in the hospital, I write from personal experience as well. In all of this, Jesus in the Blessed Sacrament has been my Joy, Delight and Strength.

May the words contained in this booklet bring hope, comfort and peace to the sick and all honor and glory to Eucharistic Jesus.

Penny Hickey, OCDS
Boiling Springs, Pennsylvania
August 1998

Table of Contents

General Illnesses

Once, when Peter and John were going up to the temple for prayer at the three o'clock hour, a man crippled from birth was being carried in. They would bring him every day and put him at the temple gate called "the Beautiful" to beg from the people as they entered. When he saw Peter and John on their way in, he begged them for an alms. Peter fixed his gaze on the man; so did John. "Look at us!" Peter said. The cripple gave them his whole attention, hoping to get something. Then Peter said: "I have neither silver nor gold, but what I have I give you! In the name of Jesus Christ the Nazorean, walk!" Then Peter took him by the right hand and pulled him up. Immediately the beggar's feet and ankles became strong; he jumped up, stood for a moment, then began to walk around. He went into the temple with them—walking, jumping about, and praising God.

Acts 3:1-8

General Illness

Sweet Jesus, Joy of our morning, Delight of our day, thank You for coming from Heaven to be with [name]. When You come You bring gifts more precious than silver or gold. You give us Your whole Being— Body, Blood, Soul and Divinity. Just as the beggar was healed, please pour out your healing love on Your dear friend today. Bless the doctors, nurses and therapists. Let them be gentle and compassionate sources of Your healing love. Fill this day with Your Presence and Your blessing.

"If sometimes bitter suffering
Should come to visit your heart,
Make it your joy:
To suffer for God . . . what sweetness!
Then Divine Tenderness
Will make you soon forget
That you walk on thorns."

St. Therese of Lisieux
Love in the Heart of the Church

Jesus toured all of Galilee. He taught in their synagogues, proclaimed the good news of the kingdom,
and cured the people of every disease and illness. As
a consequence of this, his reputation traveled the
length of Syria. They carried to him all those afflicted
with various diseases and racked with pain. . . . He
cured them all.

Mt 4:23, 24

General
(in winter)

O Precious Jesus, thank You for coming to be with [name]. Thank You for this beautiful morning all decked with snow. The spotless white reminds us of the Sacred Host. The stillness speaks loudly of Your Presence. May each snowflake be a sign of Your Love to Your child who suffers. May the warmth of Your Heart dispel the cold of winter, and bring Your healing and peace. You know all of [name's] hopes, fears, needs and desires and we entrust them to Your Loving Sacred Heart asking You to hear and answer them. Amen.

"My heaven is hidden in the little Host where Jesus, my Spouse, hides Himself through love."

St. Therese of Lisieux
Spiritual Realism of St. Therese of Lisieux

After making the crossing they reached the shore at Gennesaret; and when the men of that place recognized him they spread the word throughout the region. People brought him all the afflicted, with the plea that he let them do no more than touch the tassel of his cloak. As many as touched it were fully restored to health.

Mt 14:34-36

General

Jesus, You are our joy and our life! Thank You for coming to dwell in [name's] heart. How eagerly Your loved one looks forward to Your coming. You bring consolation and relief from suffering. You also bear spiritual gifts so subtle that they often go unnoticed at the time. How noble a Guest! As You walked the earth people brought You the sick, blind and lame and You healed them. Now You go about seeking out those who need Your help; and You still comfort and heal them. Therefore, we confidently ask You for healing for [name] as only You can provide.

"I believe the matter is very clear: the Lord is present in the tabernacle in his divinity and in his humanity. He is not present for his own sake but for ours; it is his delight to be with the 'children of men.' He knows, too, that, being what we are, we need his personal nearness."

St. Edith Stein
Self Portrait in Letters

"Ask, and you will receive. Seek, and you will find. Knock, and it will be opened to you. For the one who asks, receives. The one who seeks, finds. The one who knocks, enters. Would one of you hand his son a stone when he asks for a loaf, or a poisonous snake when he asks for a fish? If you, with all your sins, know how to give your children what is good, how much more will your heavenly Father give good things to anyone who asks him!"

Mt 7:7-11

General

Sweet Jesus, You tell us to ask, seek, knock and we shall receive. What Manner of a God are You to encourage Your little ones to ask for what they need no matter how great or how trivial? It seems to be Your pleasure to lavish gifts on Your people. Today I come asking, seeking, knocking that Your friend [name] may be healed. Please bless [him, her] with Your healing and restoration of body, mind and spirit. Because we trust in You, we thank You at the same time we ask.

"The art of sanctity consists in welcoming suffering as God's gift: the divine Crucified inoculates us with His love through the wounds of our body and our spirit. Sister Mary of Jesus Crucified suffered, she said, because 'Love is not loved.' This is the cry of all souls in love with the God of Love."

Bl. Mary of Jesus Crucified
Mariam: "The Little Arab"

Then he reentered the boat, made the crossing, and came back to his own town. There the people at once brought to him a paralyzed man lying on a mat. When Jesus saw their faith he said to the paralytic, "Have courage, son, your sins are forgiven."

At that some of the scribes said to themselves, "The man blasphemes." Jesus was aware of what they were thinking and said: "Why do you harbor evil thoughts? Which is less trouble to say, 'Your sins are forgiven' or ' Stand up and walk'? To help you realize that the Son of Man has authority on earth to forgive sins"—then he said to the paralyzed man—"Stand up! Roll up your mat and go home." The man stood up, and went toward his home. At the sight, a feeling of awe came over the crowd, and they praised God. . . .

Mt 9:1-8

General
(Rainy Day)

S weet Jesus, thank You for another day to praise You and love You! Your friend [name] is sick and dreads another day of suffering. Even the rain seems to add to the suffering. Let each raindrop be a blessing falling to the earth, especially for [name]. You have come to console your afflicted one. By this Holy Sacrament bring Your healing love and restore not only this fragile body, but [his, her] whole being. Protect Your dear one from a spirit of discouragement, and fill [him, her] with a holy hope.

St. Teresa recalling a woman healed by the Eucharist: "When she heard some persons saying that they would have liked to have lived at the time of Christ. . . . She wondered what more they wanted since in the most Blessed Sacrament they had Him just as truly present as He was then."

St Teresa of Avila
Collected Works of St. Teresa of Avila, Vol. II

Prolonged Illnesses

For we do not have a high priest who is unable to sympathize with our weakness, but one who was tempted in every way that we are, yet never sinned. So let us confidently approach the throne of grace to receive mercy and favor and to find help in time of need.

Heb 4:15, 16

Prolonged Illness

O Jesus, Calvary seems so distant in time and space, but Your friend [name] is sharing in it right now. These sufferings seem so lengthy and so futile, but in Your eyes they are of infinite value. [Name] has suffered patiently for numerous days and finds no relief. Please let drops of Your Precious Blood fall on Your child to bring healing. As [name] continues to wait for complete healing let this time be used to draw closer to You. Let it be a retreat time spent in union with You.

On the day of her first Communion Therese markedly experienced the love of Jesus. In her memoirs she wrote: "For a long time Jesus and Therese had looked at and understood each other. That day it was no longer a look but a fusion. They were no longer two; Therese had disappeared like a drop of water lost in the depths of the ocean. Jesus alone remained. He was the Master, the King. Had not Therese asked Him to take away the liberty that frightened her? She felt herself so weak and frail that she wanted to be forever united to Divine Strength!"

St. Therese of Lisieux
Story of a Soul

He told them a parable on the necessity of praying always and not losing heart: "Once there was a judge in a certain city who respected neither God nor man. A widow in that city kept coming to him saying, 'Give me my rights against my opponent.' For a time he refused, but finally he thought, 'I care little for God or man, but this widow is wearing me out. I am going to settle in her favor or she will end by doing me violence.'"

The Lord said, "Listen to what the corrupt judge has to say. Will not God then do justice to his chosen who call out to him day and night? Will he delay long over them, do you suppose? I tell you, he will give them swift justice. But when the Son of Man comes, will he find any faith on the earth?"

Lk 18:1-8

Prolonged Illness

O Jesus, Your friend [name] has been ill for so long. It is easy for Your little one to become discouraged now that faith is being tested. It would seem that You are not hearing these pleas. But we come asking You again to pour out Your healing love on [him, her]. Your Gospel speaks of the woman who persisted in petitioning the unjust judge and won in the end. You Who are justice and mercy, how much more will You hear the cries of Your little ones! As [name] waits for this healing, please grant patience, hope and confidence in You.

"That he expected, after the pleasant days God had given him, he should have his turn of pain and suffering; but that he was not uneasy about it, knowing very well that as he could do nothing of himself, God would not fail to give him the strength to bear it. That when an occasion of practicing some virtue offered, he addressed himself to God, saying, *Lord, I cannot do this unless You enable me*; and that then he received grace more than sufficient."

Br. Lawrence of the Resurrection
Practice of the Presence of God

I for my part am already being poured out like a libation. The time of my dissolution is near. I have fought the good fight, I have finished the race, I have kept the faith.

2 Tm 4:6, 7

Prolonged Illness
(morning)

O Jesus, thank You for the gloriously beautiful sunrise this morning! It was a real sign of Your Powerful Presence in the world. In spite of many treatments Your friend continues to suffer. [Name] unites all of the suffering with Yours. Please, Jesus, do not let any of these sufferings be wasted, but let them be a cause for many souls to return to You. May this Holy Sacrament give strength and courage to [name] to persevere in hope, because of Your love and mercy. May the sunshine remind Your dear one of Your loving care throughout the day.

"We object when he [God] hands us the chalice of his suffering. It is so difficult for us to resign ourselves to suffering. To rejoice in it strikes us as heroic. What is the value of our offering of self if we unite ourselves each morning only in word and gesture, rather than in thought and will, to that offering which we, together with the Church, make of him with whom we are one body? Oh, that this day we might realize the value God has placed on the suffering he sends: he, the All-Good."

Bl. Titus Brandsma, OCD
Carmelite Proper of the Liturgy of the Hours

As they were going, a woman who had suffered from hemorrhages for twelve years came up behind him and touched the tassel on his cloak. "If only I can touch his cloak," she thought, "I shall get well." Jesus turned around and saw her and said, "Courage, daughter! Your faith has restored you to health." That very moment the woman got well.

Mt 9:20-22

Prolonged Illness

J esus, in Your Gospel You speak of the woman with the hemorrhage who had suffered many years and been treated by many doctors. One touch of Your cloak and she was healed. Today You have come to [name]. You have more than touched Your child, You have come to dwell in [him, her]. In spite of treatment by so many doctors, Your friend still lingers in this illness. [Name's] faith is so great that You are welcomed eagerly each morning. Say but the word and [he, she] will be healed!

"Since we know that Jesus is with us as long as the natural heat doesn't consume the accidents of bread, we should approach Him. Now, then, if when He went about in the world the mere touch of His robes cured the sick, why doubt, if we have faith, that miracles will be worked while He is within us and that He will give what we ask of Him, since He is in our house? His Majesty is not accustomed to paying poorly for His lodging if the hospitality is good."

St. Teresa of Avila
Collected Works of St. Teresa of Avila, Vol. II

Specific Illnesses

But I am afflicted and in pain;
 let your saving help, O God, protect me.
I will praise the name of God in song,
 and I will glorify him with thanksgiving.

Ps 69:30, 31

Accident

Sweet Jesus, thank You for sparing [name's] life in the accident. The memory of that tragic time remains, and the scars run deeper than the surface. Remind Your loved one that You were there with [him, her] in the accident, and that You always will be there in the future. Fill this day with new healing, and tangible signs of recovery. As You come to [name] soothe, comfort and bless each wound.

"We look at ourselves too much, we want to see and understand, we do not have enough confidence in Him Who envelops us in His Love. We must not stop before the Cross and regard it in itself, but recollecting ourselves in the light of faith, we must rise higher and think that it is the instrument which is obeying divine Love."

Bl. Elizabeth of the Trinity
Light Love Life

O God, you are my God whom I seek;
  for you my flesh pines and my soul thirsts
  like the earth, parched, lifeless and without water.
Thus have I gazed toward you in the sanctuary
  to see your power and your glory.
For your kindness is a greater good than life;
  my lips shall glorify you.

Ps 63:2-4

Addiction

Sweet Jesus, [name] suffers so much because of an addiction. Please restore any organs that have been damaged; especially heal the deep wounds in the heart. You know the hidden emptiness and longing that Your friend feels with this addiction. Heal the pain and replace this substance with Your Very Self. You alone are our Joy and Peace! In moments of temptation or weakness let [name] run to You and find strength.

"If we don't want to be fools and blind the intellect there's no reason for doubt. Receiving Communion is not like picturing with the imagination, as when we reflect upon the Lord on the cross or in other episodes of the Passion, when we picture within ourselves how things happened to Him in the past. In Communion the event is happening now, and it is entirely true. There's no reason to go looking for Him in some other place far away."

St. Teresa of Avila
Collected Works of St. Teresa of Avila, Vol. II

You who dwell in the shelter of the Most High,
  who abide in the shadow of the Almighty,
Say to the LORD, "My refuge and my fortress,
  my God, in whom I trust."
For he will rescue you from the snare of the fowler,
  from the destroying pestilence.
With his pinions he will cover you,
  and under his wings you shall take refuge;
his faithfulness is a buckler and a shield.

Ps 91:1-4

AIDS

J esus, hidden in this tiny Host, You come to be with all Your children. You come in gentleness and humility to bring health and hope to those who cry out to You. You healed all manner of diseases as You walked the earth. Please touch and heal Your friend [name] who suffers from AIDS. May Your Presence reveal Your tender love and compassion. If others shrink from serving You in Your friend, You will never abandon [him, her]. Inspire researchers to find a cure for this dreaded disease. Through this illness may Your child draw ever nearer to You.

"O my God, since seeking You demands a heart, naked, strong and free from all evils and goods that are not purely You, help me not to gather the flowers I see along the way, nor pay heed to the gratifications, satisfactions and delights that may be offered to me in this life, and which may hinder me on the way. I will not set my heart on the riches and goods the world offers, neither will I tolerate the delights of my flesh, nor pay heed to the satisfactions and consolations of my spirit in a way that may detain me from seeking my Love in the mountains of virtues and trials. And finally, if it be possible, grant, O Lord, that my soul may be truly loving, esteeming You above all things, trusting in Your love and friendship."

St. John of the Cross
Divine Intimacy, Vol. III

"I am the bread of life.
Your ancestors ate manna in the desert,
  but they died.
This is the bread that comes down from heaven
for a man to eat and never die.
I myself am the living bread come down from
  heaven.
If anyone eats this bread
he shall live forever;
the bread I will give
is my flesh, for the life of the world."

Jn 6:48-51

Anorexia

O Jesus Most Delectable Food of the sick, weary, needy we welcome You this morning. Your friend [name] is sick and unable to eat. Even when no other food is palatable, You fill all our needs. How many Saints have lived on You Alone! May this Holy Sacrament, the Bread of Life, sustain and nourish [name]. May It bring complete healing for Your honor and glory, and satisfy every spiritual longing.

Bl. Elizabeth of the Trinity declares: "Neither trials from without or from within can make her leave the fortress in which her Master has enclosed her. She no longer feels 'hunger or thirst,' for in spite of her consuming desire for Beatitude, she is satisfied by this food that was her Master's: 'The will of the Father.' She no longer suffers from suffering. Then the Lamb can 'lead her to the fountain of life,' where He wills, as He wills, for she does not look at the paths on which she is walking, she simply gazes at the Shepherd who is leading her."

Bl. Elizabeth of the Trinity
Light Love Light

On a sabbath day he was teaching in one of the synagogues. There was a woman there who for eighteen years had been possessed by a spirit which drained her strength. She was badly stooped—quite incapable of standing erect. When Jesus saw her, he called her to him and said, "Woman, you are free of your infirmity." He laid his hand on her, and immediately she stood up straight and began thanking God.

Lk 13:10-13

Back Pain

S weet Jesus, Your friend [name's] back is so painful. You suffered from excruciating pain in Your scourging and when stretched out on the Cross. You well understand unrelenting pain. Please send Your angels to lift up and ease the suffering of Your child. Send Our Lady to be [his, her] "nurse." She will be Comforter and Mother. Just as You freed the woman who suffered from a crippling back deformity for eighteen years, pour out Your healing love on [name], and relieve the agony that seems so interminable.

"God gives me courage in proportion to my sufferings. I feel at this moment I couldn't suffer any more, but I'm not afraid, since if they increase, He will increase my courage at the same time."

St. Therese of Lisieux
Love in the Heart of the Church

Thereupon Jesus said to them:
"Let me solemnly assure you,
if you do not eat the flesh of the Son of Man
and drink his blood,
you have no life in you.
He who feeds on my flesh
and drinks my blood
has life eternal
and I will raise him up on the last day.
For my flesh is real food
and my blood real drink."

Jn 6:53-55

Blood Disorder

O Jesus, You have given us so many proofs of Your Real Presence in the Blessed Sacrament. You have even allowed Your Miraculous Hosts and Precious Blood to be tested. How patient You are! Sweet Jesus, Your friend [name] suffers with a disorder of the blood. As You come today unite Your Blood with [his, hers]. You be the Transfusion and let Your Blood replace the diseased blood. May this Eucharistic Healing be for Your honor and glory.

One Carmelite testified of Bl. Mary of Jesus Crucified: "I have seen her returning to her place after receiving Communion, fall hard on her knees saying energetically: 'Now I have everything.'"

Bl. Mary of Jesus Crucified
Mariam: "The Little Arab"

The spirit of the Lord God is upon me,
  because the Lord has anointed me;
He has sent me to bring glad tidings to the lowly,
  to heal the brokenhearted,
To proclaim liberty to the captives
  and release to the prisoners,
To announce a year of favor from the LORD
  and a day of vindication by our God,
  to comfort all who mourn;
To place on those who mourn in Zion
  a diadem instead of ashes,
To give them oil of gladness in place of mourning,
  a glorious mantle instead of a listless spirit,
They will be called oaks of justice,
  planted by the LORD to show his glory.

Is 61:1-3

Coma

O Dear Jesus, Your friend lies in a coma. It is not possible for Your little one to express any prayers or needs. I bring your presence in the Eucharist to [name] and ask You to come spiritually into [his, her] soul and remain there always. May the angels come and sing sweetly at this bedside, and Our Lady stand guard too. Please bring healing and restoration, O Dear Doctor of body and soul! Flood [name] with Your peace and awaken Your child to a new day in Your light.

"Let all my care be directed toward how I may give you some pleasure and render you some service because of what you deserve and the favors you have bestowed on me, even though the cost may be high. . . . Ah my Lord and my God, how many go to you looking for their own consolation and gratification, your favors and gifts, while those who want to give you pleasure and something at a cost to themselves, setting aside their own interests, are so few! My Beloved, all that is rugged and toilsome I desire for myself, and all that is sweet and delightful I desire for you."

St. John of the Cross
Divine Intimacy, Vol. III

Bless the LORD, O my soul;
  and all my being, bless his holy name.
Bless the LORD, O my soul,
  and forget not all his benefits;
He pardons all your iniquities,
  he heals all your ills.
He redeems your life from destruction,
  he crowns you with kindness and compassion,
He fills your lifetime with good;
  your youth is renewed like the eagle's.

Ps 103:1-5

Heart

Sweet Jesus, You have come to be with [name]. Your child's heart is weak and [he, she] is weary. You know how vulnerable Your children feel when their heart is afflicted. May the wound in Your Sacred Heart open wide and spill out Your Precious Blood with Its healing love. As You come in this Holy Sacrament unite this weakened heart with Yours, supplying new life and strength. Touch [name] so that this union of hearts will manifest Your Mercy to all the world.

"Prayer is the heart of man in the heart of God, it is the eyes of a poor being loving in the eyes of God; it is the silent soul, wordless before God, bent eagerly toward God, melting with love before God, wearying of its God, weeping with weariness of God, frightfully tormented by a terrible hunger for God and seeking in the flight of its outpouring to seize God, to embrace Him, to embrace Him without end."

Fr. Jacques Bunel, OCD
Pere Jacques, Spiritual Guide

When I call, answer me, O my just God,
  you who relieve me when I am in distress;
Have pity on me, and hear my prayer!

Many say, "Oh, that we might see better times!"
  O LORD, let the light of your countenance shine
    upon us!
You put gladness into my heart,
  more than when grain and wine abound.
As soon as I lie down, I fall peacefully asleep,
  for you alone, O LORD,
  bring security to my dwelling.

Ps 4:2, 7-9

Insomnia

O Jesus, You never slumber or sleep. You are always there whenever we call You. Your friend [name] is so weary from a restless night. You spent a long lonely night in Your Agony in the Garden, and You can well sympathize. Please refresh Your dear one with Your Holy Sacrament and send Our Lady to watch over her child. May she mother [name], and keep her little one company in the long hours of the night.

In her writings Blessed Elizabeth of the Trinity reveals of herself: "Your little praise of glory cannot sleep; she suffers very much, but in her soul, although the anguish penetrates there too, she feels such peace. . . . I feel my Three so close to me; I am more overwhelmed by happiness than by pain."

Bl. Elizabeth of the Trinity
Light Love Life

He got into the boat and his disciples followed him. Without warning a violent storm came up on the lake, and the boat began to be swamped by the waves. Jesus was sleeping soundly, so they made their way toward him and woke him: "Lord, save us! We are lost!" He said to them, "Where is your courage? How little faith you have!" Then he stood up and took the winds and the sea to task. Complete calm ensued; the men were dumbfounded. "What sort of man is this," they said, "that even the winds and the sea obey him?"

Mt 8:23-27

Lungs

O Jesus, You calm all the storms in our lives! Your friend [name] is struggling for a breath, and is so frightened. You are as truly present here as You were with the disciples in the boat. May You be [his, her] Breath of Life. Restore peace with Your Presence; never let Your friend be engulfed in the waves of fear and doubt. Please breathe on [name] and make [him, her] whole.

"O Christ crucified. You are enough for me, with You I desire to suffer and find rest. . . . Crucified inwardly and outwardly with You, may I live in this life with fullness and satisfaction of soul, and possess my soul in patience. Grant me a great love for trials and help me to think of them as but a small way of pleasing You, O Lord, Who did not hesitate to die for me."

St John of the Cross
Divine Intimacy, Vol. IV

As evening drew on, they brought him many who were possessed. He expelled the spirits by a simple command and cured all who were afflicted, thereby fulfilling what had been said through Isaiah the prophet:

"It was our infirmities he bore,
   our sufferings he endured."

Mt 8:16, 17

Multiple Infirmities

O Jesus, Your friend [name] suffers from head to foot. Many are the infirmities. As I gaze on Your suffering servant I am reminded of all You endured in Your Passion. How much You love [name] that You share Your Cross with [him, her]. Show Your child how to apply these sufferings in union with Yours in the great plan of Redemption. Hold [name] close to You and never let [his, her] hope in You fail. May the wound in Your Heart, Dear Jesus, open wide and spill out Your healing love.

"Suffering borne in union with Christ is His suffering, inserted in the great work of Redemption and bearing fruit in it."

St. Edith Stein
Reflections

He then left Tyrian territory and returned by way of Sidon to the Sea of Galilee, into the district of the Ten Cities. Some people brought him a deaf man who had a speech impediment and begged him to lay his hand on him.

Jesus took him off by himself away from the crowd. He put his fingers into the man's ears and, spitting, touched his tongue; then he looked up to heaven and emitted a groan. He said to him, "*Ephphatha!*" (that is, "Be opened!") At once the man's ears were opened; he was freed from the impediment, and began to speak plainly.

Mk 7:31-35

Speech

O Sweet Jesus, Your friend [name] struggles to speak and to be understood. We thank You for the gift of our senses. You have given us not only the ability to speak with our tongue, but with our writing, our actions and even our eyes. No words are necessary to speak with You. You know all our thoughts and even all our secrets. Your child so desires to be able to speak, so as You come today please touch and loose [his, her] tongue to sing Your praises forever.

"For is there a greater joy than that of suffering out of love for You? The more interior the suffering is and the less apparent to the eyes of creatures the more it rejoices You, O my God! But if my suffering was really unknown to You, which is impossible, I would still be happy to have it, if through it I could prevent or make reparation for one single sin against faith."

St. Therese of Lisieux
Story of a Soul

Where can I go from your spirit?
   from your presence where can I flee?
If I go up to the heavens, you are there;
   if I sink to the nether world, you are present there.
If I take the wings of the dawn,
   if I settle at the farthest limits of the sea,
Even there your hand shall guide me,
   and your right hand hold me fast.
If I say, "Surely the darkness shall hide me,
   and night shall be my light"—
For you darkness itself is not dark,
   and night shines as the day.
   [Darkness and light are the same.]

Truly you have formed my inmost being;
   you knit me in my mother's womb.
I give you thanks that I am fearfully,
      wonderfully made;
   wonderful are your works.

                                        Ps 139:7-14

Undetermined Illness

O Sweet Jesus, Your friend [name] is sick and suffering with an undetermined illness. The tests and treatments are so wearisome and produce no diagnosis. You Who created [him, her] know all the secrets of the body and this sickness as well. You also know the perfect remedy. Please lay Your healing hand on [him, her] and restore health of body, mind and spirit.

"Since God does not distribute his graces to men except through prayer, because he wishes us to recognize him as the source from which all good things flow; in like manner, he does not wish to save us from danger, or cure our wounds, or console us in affliction, except by means of this same exercise of prayer."

Bl. Francis Palau y Quer
Carmelite Proper of the Liturgy of the Hours

As Jesus moved on from there, two blind men came after him crying out, "Son of David, have pity on us!" When he got to the house, the blind men caught up with him. Jesus said to them, "Are you confident I can do this?" "Yes, Lord," they told him. At that he touched their eyes, and said, "Because of your faith it shall be done to you"; and they recovered their sight.

Mt 9:27-30

Vision

Dear Jesus, Your friend [name] cries out to be able to see. You have created a world of beauty that so many who are able to see do not see. Your friend who is blind sees so much with the eyes of the soul, but still yearns to see with physical eyes. May the eyes of Your child's soul never become dimmed to the sight of You, and by this Holy Sacrament please restore the physical sight that has been lost.

"O how we fail to know what we are asking for; and how His wisdom provides in a better way! He reveals Himself to those whom He sees will benefit by His presence. Even though they fail to see Him with their bodily eyes, He has many methods of showing Himself to the soul, through great interior feelings and other different ways. Be with Him willingly; don't lose so good an occasion for conversing with Him as is the hour after having received Communion."

St. Teresa of Avila
Collected Works of St. Teresa of Avila, Vol. II

Emotional/Spiritual

I will not leave you orphaned;
I will come back to you.
A little while now and the world will see me no
  more;
but you see me
as one who has life, and you will have life.
On that day you will know
that I am in my Father,
and you in me, and I in you.

Jn 14:18-20

Abandonment

S weet Jesus, Your beloved friend is so grief stricken, and feels abandoned. When all our friends and family are absent and we seem to be alone, we are not alone. You never leave us or cease to love and provide for us. Please reveal Your Presence to [name]. Speak to [his, her] heart, and heal the wounds of this abandonment. You Alone can fill all our dark nights and all voids. You are Everything Good!

"If men only knew how to discover His invisible, ceaseless Presence, and if only they knew how to live with Him in a peaceful intercourse of friendship, what unutterable happiness they would savor, a happiness so calm and beneficent. What is suffering when it is enveloped in this infinity of love?"

Fr. Jacques Bunel, OCD
Pere Jacques, Spiritual Guide

"I warn you, then: do not worry about your livelihood, what you are to eat or drink or use for clothing. Is not life more than food? Is not the body more valuable than clothes? Look at the birds in the sky. They do not sow or reap, they gather nothing into barns; yet your heavenly Father feeds them. Are you not more important than they? Which of you by worrying can add a moment to his life-span?"

Mt 6:25-27

Feels Like a Burden

Sweet Jesus, Your friend [name] is feeling such a burden on those who care for [him, her]. Please let this loved child know the infinite value each life has in Your eyes. Please enable [name] to see that this suffering in union with Yours is of great merit. Remind Your friend too, that we must become like little children to enter Your heavenly Kingdom. Dry [his, her] tears and by Your grace bring resignation to Your Will with much joy in fulfilling It!

"Mother, what touches me above all else is the novena you are making at Our Lady of Victories, I mean the Masses you are having offered up to obtain my cure. I feel all these spiritual treasures do great good to my soul; at the commencement of the Novena I told you the Blessed Virgin would have to cure me or carry me off to heaven because I find it very sad for you and the community to have to take care of a young sick religious. But now I would want to be sick all my life if this pleased God, and I even consent to my life being very long; the only favor I desire is that it be broken through love."

St. Therese of Lisieux
Story of a Soul

But I refrain, lest anyone think more of me than what he sees in me or hears from my lips. As to the extraordinary revelations, in order that I might not become conceited I was given a thorn in the flesh, an angel of Satan to beat me and keep me from getting proud. Three times I begged the Lord that this might leave me. He said to me, "My grace is enough for you, for in weakness power reaches perfection." And so I willingly boast of my weaknesses instead, that the power of Christ may rest upon me.

Therefore I am content with weakness, with mistreatment, with distress, with persecutions and difficulties for the sake of Christ; for when I am powerless, it is then that I am strong.

2 Cor 12:7-10

Helpless

Dear Jesus, I bring You Your friend [name] who is no longer able to be independent, and is feeling so helpless. You Yourself have experienced helplessness, Beloved Jesus. You came to earth as a tiny Infant even though You are God. You also were delivered into the hands of Your executioners for love of us. You hide within the Sacred Host and put Yourself at the disposal of good and bad alike. You understand perfectly what Your dear one suffers. Please let Your lamb know how much You love [him, her]. We are told in Scripture that when we are weak You are strong. Please help and protect Your [brother, sister name]. Carry Your dear one in Your arms close to Your Heart.

"Abandonment—that is what surrenders us to God. I am quite young, but it seems to me that I have suffered much sometimes. Oh, then, when everything was dark, when the present was so painful and the future seemed even more gloomy to me, I closed my eyes and abandoned myself like a child in the arms of this Heavenly Father."

Bl. Elizabeth of the Trinity
Light Love Life

O LORD, my heart is not proud,
  nor are my eyes haughty;
I busy not myself with great things,
  nor with things too sublime for me.
Nay rather, I have stilled and quieted
  my soul like a weaned child.
Like a weaned child on its mother's lap,
  [so is my soul within me.]
  O Israel, hope in the LORD,
  both now and forever.

Ps 131

Hopeless

Sweet Jesus, You have come to be with [name] who is feeling so hopeless. This dear friend feels You have abandoned [him, her]. Your Very Presence in this Holy Sacrament proves Your constant love. Please lift [name] up to Your Heart and in Your mercy hear the cries of Your child. Let [name] know You are near and that You love [him, her] immensely! You alone are Hope of the hopeless and our Dearest Treasure.

Lesson learned by Br. Lawrence from his prayer with Jesus: "That all things are possible to him who *believes*; that they are less difficult to him who *hopes*; that they are more easy to him who *loves* and still more easy to him who perseveres in the practice of these three virtues."

Br. Lawrence of the Resurrection
Practice of the Presence of God

I lift up my eyes toward the mountains;
   whence shall help come to me?
My help is from the LORD,
   who made heaven and earth.

May he not suffer your foot to slip;
   may he slumber not who guards you:
Indeed he neither slumbers nor sleeps,
   the guardian of Israel.

The LORD is your guardian; the LORD is your
      shade;
   he is beside you at your right hand.
The sun shall not harm you by day,
   nor the moon by night.

The LORD will guard you from all evil;
   he will guard your life.
The LORD will guard your coming and your going,
   both now and forever.

                                    Ps 121

Injured by Another

O Gentle Jesus, I bring You [name]. Your little one has been so battered and neglected. Let Your child find refuge in You. Let [name] know You were there grieving during the abuse; and that what was done to [him, her] was done to You. Gather Your lamb into Your arms and replace this spirit of fear with Your spirit of peace and hope! Let [name] know of Your unfailing love.

"I unite myself to Jesus when He was carrying His cross in the streets of Jerusalem. May You be blessed my God. I unite my voice with that of Jesus in the Garden of Olives. May You be blessed, my God. I unite my sufferings to those of Jesus betrayed by Judas. May You be blessed, my God. I unite myself to Jesus falling under the weight of the cross. May You be blessed, my God."

Bl. Mary of Jesus Crucified
Mariam: "The Little Arab"

Where can I go from your spirit?
  from your presence where can I flee?
If I go up to the heavens, you are there;
  if I sink to the nether world, you are present there.
If I take the wings of the dawn,
  if I settle at the farthest limits of the sea,
Even there your hand shall guide me,
  and your right hand hold me fast.

Ps 139:7-10

Lonely

My Jesus, Your friend is feeling so alone and so isolated. Please let [name] know that [he, she] is not alone, but that You are always there. Please send holy angels and Our Lady to be dear companions. Send Your people to visit and bring Your love. May [name] know that Your love is immense and eternal, and that You will never leave [him, her] abandoned. You are only a thought, a prayer, a sigh away. Who could find a more Loving Friend!

"How great is the power of prayer! . . . To be heard it is not necessary to read from a book some beautiful formula composed for the occasion. . . . I say very simply to God what I wish to say, without composing beautiful sentences, and He always understands me. For me, prayer is an aspiration of the heart, it is a simple glance directed to heaven, it is a cry of gratitude and love in the midst of trial as well as joy; finally, it is something great, supernatural, that expands my soul and unites me to Jesus."

St. Therese of Lisieux
Story of a Soul

Incline your ear, O LORD, answer me,
  for I am afflicted and poor.
Keep my life, for I am devoted to you;
  save your servant who trusts in you.
You are my God; have pity on me, O Lord,
  for to you I call all the day.
Gladden the soul of your servant,
  for to you, O Lord, I lift up my soul;
For you, O Lord, are good and forgiving,
  abounding in kindness to all who
  call upon you.

Ps 86:1-5

Mercy

Sweet Jesus, You are all love and mercy. Your mercy led You to Calvary for poor sinners, and Your sacrifice continues daily in the Mass. Your friend [name] is so distressed, filled with anger and bitterness. You know the pain this is causing [name]. Replace this anger with Your spirit of love and mercy. Heal the wounds of this poor [man's, woman's] soul and bring wholeness of body, mind and spirit as You come in Holy Communion.

Bakanja Isidore, a native of Zaire and a member of the Scapular Confraternity, died because he did not want to remove his scapular. When his atheist employer ordered him to take off his scapular, he refused. As a result he received floggings that left incurable wounds on his back.

The following six and a half months that he lived in torment were more painful than the beatings themselves. When the missionaries were giving him the last Sacraments they asked him to pardon the man who had beaten him. He replied, "I have already pardoned him and when I am in heaven I intend to pray for him too."

Carmel Clarion

"'Peace' is my farewell to you,
my peace is my gift to you;
I do not give it to you as the world gives peace.
Do not be distressed or fearful."

Jn 14:27

Painful Memories

O Jesus, Your friend [name] is suffering from memories of past terrors. Help [him, her] to live in the gift of the present moment. Please let Your dear one know that the past is gone and that You are already there in the future. Help Your child to accept the gift of peace that You offer right now. Heal those painful memories, Sweet Jesus, for You are all love.

"O my God, Trinity whom I adore, help me to forget myself entirely that I may be established in You as still and as peaceful as if my soul were already in eternity. May nothing trouble my peace or make me leave You, O my Unchanging One, but may each minute carry me further into the depths of Your Mystery. Give peace to my soul; make it Your heaven, Your beloved dwelling and Your resting place. May I never leave You there alone, but be wholly present, my faith wholly vigilant, wholly adoring, and wholly surrendered to Your creative action."

Bl. Elizabeth of the Trinity
Light Love Life

Jesus said to them, "The healthy do not need a doctor; sick people do. I have not come to invite the self-righteous to a change of heart, but sinners."

Lk 5:31, 32

Fear of Past Sins

Sweet Jesus, Your friend [name] is suffering and feels that this illness is caused or deserved because of past sins. You did not come to punish sinners, but to save them. Please let [name] know of Your great love for [him, her]; and that You seek out the lost sheep to bring them home. You knew we would need healing and have provided so perfectly in this Sacrament of Holy Communion and the Sacrament of Reconciliation. Let [name] know that You are truly meek and gentle of heart.

"I consider myself as the most wretched of men, full of sores and corruption, and who has committed all sorts of crimes against his King. Touched with a sensible regret, I confess to Him all my wickedness, I ask His forgiveness, I abandon myself in His hands that He may do what He pleases with me. The King, full of mercy and goodness, very far from chastising me, embraces me with love, makes me eat at His table, serves me with His own hands, gives me the key of His treasures; He converses and delights Himself with me incessantly, in thousands and thousands of ways, and treats me in all respects as His favorite."

Br. Lawrence of the Resurrection
Practice of the Presence of God

Persons

Before Jesus had finished speaking to them, a synagogue leader came up, did him reverence, and said: "My daughter has just died. Please come and lay your hand on her and she will come back to life." Jesus stood up and followed him, and his disciples did the same. . . . When Jesus arrived at the synagogue leader's house and saw the flute players and the crowd who were making a din, he said, "Leave, all of you! The little girl is not dead. She is asleep." At this they began to ridicule him. When the crowd had been put out he entered and took her by the hand, and the little girl got up.

Mt 9:18, 19, 23-25.

Child

Sweet Jesus, please help this poor mother and father who stand at their sick child's bedside. They feel so helpless and sad. Just as You raised the little girl when You prayed, "Little girl, arise!" please lay Your hand on [name] to restore perfect health. May Your Mother and St. Joseph come and support these loving parents. Let them know that You love them and are with them. May Your Holy Presence in Communion be their Consolation!

Mariam [Bl. Mary of Jesus Crucified] went to confession every Saturday, and already at the age of seven she was tortured by hunger for the Eucharist. . . . The day she first received Him she "was radiant with happiness," and later acknowledged she had seen Jesus give Himself to her under the appearance of a most beautiful Child.

Bl. Mary of Jesus Crucified
Mariam: "The Little Arab"

"See that you never despise one of these little ones. I assure you, their angels in heaven constantly behold my heavenly Father's face."

Mt 18:10, 11

Child

O my Jesus, Your little child is sick. Everything that is done to treat this little one is frightening and unfamiliar. You love the little children; please make [name] well soon. This family is full of confidence in You. Please send the angels to help [name] and Our Lady to mother [him, her] especially when these loving parents must go home. May this Communion ease the suffering not only of [name], but also the dear parents.

"Finding no help on earth, poor little Therese had also turned towards the Mother of heaven, and prayed with all her heart that She take pity on her. All of a sudden the Blessed Virgin appeared beautiful to me, so beautiful that never had I seen anything so attractive; Her face was suffused with an ineffable benevolence and tenderness, but what penetrated to the very depths of my soul was the 'ravishing smile of the Blessed Virgin.' At that instant, all my pain disappeared, and two large tears glistened on my eyelashes, and flowed down my cheeks silently, but they were tears of unmixed joy."

St. Therese of Lisieux
Story of a Soul

At the time it is administered, all discipline seems a cause for grief and not for joy, but later it brings forth the fruit of peace and justice to those who are trained in its school. So strengthen your drooping hands and your weak knees. Make straight the paths you walk on, that your halting limbs may not be dislocated but healed.

Heb 12:11-13

Elderly

J esus, we thank You for [name's] life and all the beauty that has come from it. May Your faithful one know that You dwell within. Help each faltering footstep and ease the pain of those limbs afflicted by the years of service. May this special time of [name's] life be a preparation for seeing You face to face. May these Holy Communions draw [him, her] ever closer to You.

"O my Lord! How can one ask You for favors who has so badly served You and has not known how to preserve what You have granted? How can one have confidence when she has so often betrayed You? What shall I do, Comfort of the comfortless and Remedy for those who seek help in You? Can it possibly be better for me to be silent about my necessities, hoping that You will provide a remedy for them? No, certainly not, because You, my Lord, and my Delight, knowing the many things that we need and that there is great comfort in speaking of them to You, for this reason You tell us to ask and that You will not fail to grant our requests."

St. Teresa of Avila
Lingering with My Lord

"Again I tell you, if two of you join your voices on earth to pray for anything whatever, it shall be granted you by my Father in heaven. Where two or three are gathered in my name, there am I in their midst."

Mt 18:19, 20

Married Couple

O my Jesus, this couple is suffering so much. Please remain with them. As they minister to one another may their love for one another deepen and grow. This holy love is a reminder of Your faithful love for the whole Church. Their sacred union blessed by Your hand continues to thrive, nourished by these Holy Communions. Keep them safe and send Your holy angels to help them.

"This blessed silence, this silence charged with God, is made up of deep prayer, but it does not prevent and should not hamper the duty of one's state. If one must animate all our enterprises and houses with joy, our games and activities, it must be done without harming this profound silence, for underneath the surface of a restless person, the soul ever remains in the presence of God."

Fr. Jacques Bunel, OCD
Pere Jacques, Spiritual Guide

"When a woman is in labor,
she is sad that her time has come.
When she has borne her child,
she no longer remembers her pain
for joy that a man has been born into the world."

Jn 16:21

Mother in Labor

Dear Jesus, Author of Life, please bless this expectant mother who labors to bring new life into this world. Give her courage and peace. Bless her baby; and may this child live a happy, holy life with You. May Our Lady come and assist at the delivery as she did with St. Elizabeth. Thank You for Your Real Presence at this birth through Your Holy Sacrament. What a joy! Two miracles—Your Presence and a new life!

"To those who gaze on you in your mama's arms, you seem very small, but your fond aunt who looks at you in the light of faith sees in you a nature of infinite grandeur: for from all eternity God 'has carried you in His thought; He has predestined you to be conformed to the image of His Son Jesus, and by holy Baptism He has clothed you with Himself, thus making you His children, and at the same time His living temple.' O dear little sanctuary of Love, when I see the splendor that radiates in you, and yet which is only the dawn, I fall silent and adore Him who creates such marvels."

Bl. Elizabeth of the Trinity
Light Love Life

Praised be God, the Father of our Lord Jesus Christ, the Father of mercies, and the God of all consolation! He comforts us in all our afflictions and thus enables us to comfort those who are in trouble, with the same consolation we have received from him. As we have shared much in the suffering of Christ, so through Christ do we share abundantly in his consolation.

If we are afflicted it is for your encouragement and salvation, and when we are consoled it is for your consolation, so that you may endure patiently the same sufferings we endure. Our hope for you is firm because we know that just as you share in the sufferings, so you will share in the consolation.

2 Cor 1:3-7

Priest

Jesus, Your "other self" is sick. How many people he has helped! How many blessings has he given in Your Name! How many sins has he forgiven with You! How many times he has called You to earth in Holy Communion! Thank You for allowing me to carry You to this holy Priest. How much You love him. Let those who care for him guard his dignity and bring him quickly to health. Please pour out Your blessings on him as he has done for so many.

"The prophets had already marked his [Jesus'] way of suffering; the disciples now understood that he had not avoided that way. From the crib to the cross, suffering, poverty and lack of appreciation were his lot. He had directed his whole life to teaching people how different is God's view of suffering, poverty and lack of human appreciation from the foolish wisdom of the world. After sin, suffering had to follow so that, through the cross, man's lost glory and life with God might be regained. Suffering is the way to heaven. In the cross is salvation, in the cross is victory. God willed it so."

Bl. Titus Brandsma, OCD
Carmelite Proper of the Liturgy of the Hours

[Jesus] summoned the crowd with his disciples and said to them: "If a man wishes to come after me, he must deny his very self, take up his cross, and follow in my steps. Whoever would preserve his life will lose it, but whoever loses his life for my sake and the gospel's will preserve it."

Mk 8:34, 35

Victim Soul

O Sweet Jesus, Your friend is so very ill. [Name] has offered [his, her] life as Your Victim Soul, and You have accepted. I do not ask for healing, but rather that You protect this dear lamb. Please give courage and perseverance to [name]. May St. Michael and all the angels surround this holy bed and drive away the Evil One. May Our Lady come and bring consolation and peace. Thank You, Jesus, for giving us generous souls such as [name]. Your Will be done.

"The Carmelite is a given soul,
One immolated for the glory of God.
With her Christ she is crucified.
But how luminous her Calvary!
While gazing on the Divine Victim,
A light blazed forth in her soul
And, understanding her sublime mission,
Her wounded heart exclaimed: 'Here I am!'"

Bl. Elizabeth of the Trinity
Light Love Life

Care Providers

Jesus left that place and passed along the Sea of Galilee. He went up onto the mountainside and sat down there. Large crowds of people came to him bringing with them cripples, the deformed, the blind, the mute, and many others besides. They laid them at his feet and he cured them. The result was great astonishment in the crowds as they beheld the mute speaking, the deformed made sound, cripples walking about, and the blind seeing. They glorified the God of Israel.

Mt 15:29-31

Physician

Sweet Jesus please bless [Dr. name] who receives You because of [his, her] utter dependence on You. Flood this dear doctor with Your grace, and let all the treatments prescribed be inspired by Your Holy Spirit. Let Your Sacrament of Love be the Source of caring, compassion and love [Dr. name] gives to each patient.

"O Spirit, proceeding from the Father and from the Word, You pour Yourself into the soul in so gentle a way that it is almost imperceptible, and because of its magnitude is understood by few. You infuse into the soul the power of the Father and the wisdom of the Son, and the soul, made thus so powerful and so wise, becomes capable of bearing within it so noble an inhabitant . . . causing you to rejoice in it and never to leave it."

St. Mary Magdalen de' Pazzi
Divine Intimacy, Vol. IV

"Come to me, all you who are weary and find life burdensome, and I will refresh you. Take my yoke upon your shoulders and learn from me, for I am gentle and humble of heart. Your souls will find rest, for my yoke is easy and my burden light."

Mt 11:28-30

Physician

Dear Jesus, You know how burdened and weary [Dr. name] is feeling. Your dear doctor knows [he, she] has given the best possible treatment and still the patient does not respond. Please refresh this doctor and inspire all the prescriptions through Your Holy Sacrament. May the doctor's will be one with Yours and this union bring peace.

"What can I tell you about the pain your letter brought me? How I would have loved, mother dear, to be by your side to console and weep with you. But our souls meet by the tabernacle. There let us take the bitter complaints of our heart: 'Lord, the ones who love you so much are ill.' Let us continue repeating that cry to Jesus till He is moved and brings back to life the souls for which we pray."

St. Teresa of Jesus of the Andes
Letters of St. Teresa of the Andes

Happy is he who has regard
  for the lowly and the poor;
  in the day of misfortune the L<small>ORD</small> will deliver him;
The L<small>ORD</small> will keep and preserve him;
  he will make him happy on the earth,
  and not give him over to the will of his enemies.
The L<small>ORD</small> will help him on his sickbed,
  he will take away all his ailment when he is ill.

Ps 41:2-4

Nurse

Sweet Jesus please bless [name]. Your dear one has chosen to perform works of mercy day after day. As You come today, fill [name] with patience, caring, diligence and genuine love for all the patients that You have entrusted to [him, her]. May this dear servant assist each patient as if [he, she] were caring for You.

"How I wish I had been infirmarian . . . and had her [a disagreeable Sister suffering from neurasthenia] as my patient! Grace would have spoken louder than nature, for I feel an attraction for such work. I would have put so much love into my nursing, that I am sure I would have made her happy, remembering that Our Lord said: 'I was sick and you visited Me'" (Mt 25:36).

St. Therese of Lisieux
Just For Today

Jesus entered Peter's house and found Peter's mother-in-law in bed with a fever. He took her by the hand and the fever left her. She got up at once and began to wait on him.

Mt 8:14, 15

Caregiver

O Jesus, You are all love. You stoop down from Heaven and make Yourself one with us in Your Holy Sacrament. Teach us to be kind and gentle especially when we are tried or tested. Give an extra measure of patience for each moment. May all of the little kindnesses we show be proofs of our love for You. Make us able to bring that love to all those we meet this day. At the end of this day may Your sick ones be able to feel that You Yourself visited them.

"In the light of eternity the soul sees things as they really are. Oh, how empty is all that has not been done for God and with God! I beg you, oh, mark everything with the seal of love! It alone endures."

Bl. Elizabeth of the Trinity
Light Love Life

Treatments

In him who is the source of my strength I have strength for everything.

Phil 4:13

Chemotherapy/Radiation

O Jesus, our Joy, our Consoler and Healer, [name] is undergoing chemotherapy and/or radiation. Please let the treatment blot out all the diseased cells and not harm healthy tissue. Guide the doctors, nurses, and technicians in giving the proper dosage. Please protect Your dear friend from any side effects. We come to You in confidence because You are all love and mercy.

"Do you not think this Heavenly Food fails to provide sustenance, even for these bodies, that it is not a great medicine even for bodily ills? I know that it is. I know a person with serious illnesses, who often experiences great pain, who through this Bread had them taken away as though by a gesture of the hand and was made completely well. This is a common experience."

St. Teresa of Avila
Collected Works of St. Teresa of Avila, Vol. II

Do not love money but be content with what you have, for God has said, "I will never desert you, nor will I forsake you." Thus we may say with confidence:
"The Lord is my helper,
I will not be afraid;
What can man do to me?"

Heb 13:5, 6

Surgery

Dear Jesus, Your friend [name] is facing surgery and is so filled with fear. Please calm Your child with Your Presence. Please go into surgery with [name], holding Your little one's hands and bringing a peaceful sleep. Bless the doctors' hands and let them be skillful in bringing Your healing love. Protect Your dear one in the recovery period and may this healing give You glory.

"'What shall I render unto the Lord for all that He has rendered unto me? I will take the chalice of salvation.'" Yes, O my God, if I take this chalice, crimsoned with the blood of my Master, and in utterly joyous thanksgiving, mingle my blood with that of the sacred Victim, He will impart to it something of His own infinity, and it will give You, O Father, wonderful praise. Then my suffering will become a message that will proclaim Your glory."

Bl. Elizabeth of the Trinity
Divine Intimacy, Vol. III

Death and Dying

My lover speaks; he says to me,
  "Arise my beloved, my beautiful one,
    and come!
For see, the winter is past,
  the rains are over and gone.
The flowers appear on the earth,
  the time of pruning the vines has come,
  and the song of the dove is heard in our land.
The fig tree puts forth its figs,
  and the vines, in bloom, give forth fragrance.
Arise, my beloved, my beautiful one,
  and come!"

                                    Song of Songs 2:10-13

The Dying

Jesus, in spite of the various treatments administered [name] continues to suffer and grow weaker. Your child can hear Your Dear Voice bidding [him, her] to arise and come. Let this be a cause of joy and not fear. May the angels stand guard at this bedside, and keep away the Evil One. May [he, she] hope in You who are love and mercy. Sustain the family who stand vigil and give them Your consolation. May they lay all of their tears at Your feet, and find healing there.

"Despite painful bodily suffering until the end, her [a fellow Sister] going home was extremely peaceful. Our dear patient knew from the start what was wrong with her and that there were no prospects for a cure. She offered everything for the great intentions of this time" [end of WWII].

St. Edith Stein
Self Portrait in Letters

"Eye has not seen, ear has not heard,
  nor has it so much dawned on man
  what God has prepared for those who love him."
1 Cor 2:9

The Dying

S weet Gentle Jesus, You have told us "eye has not seen, nor ear heard what You have ready for those who love You." For those who have faith, all of life is a preparation for the great moment when You will invite us to Your home. It is not the end but a glorious beginning. Please bless [name] and calm [his, her] fears. May [name] run joyfully to receive what You have prepared.

"I seem to feel myself being destroyed. . . . Sometimes it is painful for nature and I can assure you that if I were to remain at that level, I would feel only my cowardice in the face of suffering. But that is looking at things from the human point of view! Very quickly I open the eye of my soul in the light of faith. And this faith tells me that it is love Who is slowly consuming me: then I feel a tremendous joy."

Bl. Elizabeth of the Trinity
Light Love Life

Then [Jesus] went out and made his way, as was his custom, to the Mount of Olives; his disciples accompanied him. On reaching the place he said to them, "Pray that you may not be put to the test." He withdrew from them about a stone's throw, then went down on his knees and prayed in these words: "Father, if it is your will, take this cup from me; yet not my will but yours be done."

An angel then appeared to him from heaven to strengthen him. In his anguish he prayed with all the greater intensity, and his sweat became like drops of blood falling to the ground.

Lk 22:39-44

Terminal Illness

Dear Jesus, Your friend has just been told [he, she] has a terminal illness. [Name] is so fearful and sorrowful. You experienced these emotions in Your Passion and sweat blood. Please come to the aid of Your sorrowful one. Calm all fears and let this little lamb find refuge in You, Beloved Shepherd in the Eucharist. Give [him, her] hope. Nothing is impossible with You!

A Carmelite nun told Fr. Jacques Bunel that she was tormented by doubts about the Faith: "If death surprises me in this state, how will God receive me?"

Anwered Father Jacques: "But God will receive you as He received Our Lord at His death. . . . Our Lord wanted to know by experience all our sufferings, and He wanted to experience this apparent abandonment by God.

"We must love so much," he said further, "that our love, by throwing itself against this veil that hides God from us here below, spreads the meshes apart so that the rays of a pure divine light, freely darting at our soul, consume it with love."

And when the prioress expressed amazement to hear him preach on death on Easter Day, he exclaimed, "Just think, ma Mere, *to see God, to see God!*"

Fr. Jacques Bunel, OCD
Pere Jacques, Spiritual Guide

People were bringing their little children to him to have him touch them, but the disciples were scolding them for this. Jesus became indignant when he noticed it and said to them: "Let the children come to me and do not hinder them. It is to just such as these that the kingdom of God belongs. I assure you that whoever does not accept the reign of God like a little child shall not take part in it." Then he embraced them and blessed them, placing his hands on them.

Mk 10:13-16

Death of an Infant

Sweet Jesus, Comforter of those who mourn, come to this heartbroken mother who grieves for her dear baby. Please send Your sweet Mother to console her. She held Your poor Body in death and understands this terrible grief. Give [name] the grace to entrust her little one into Your hands and those of Our Lady. When [name] returns home, replace her emptiness with the love of her family and Your continuous Presence. Heal her and bless her with new life.

"Your letter gave great sadness to my soul! Poor little Papa!. . . No, the thoughts of Jesus are not our thoughts, and His ways are not our ways. . . . He is offering us a chalice as bitter as our feeble nature can bear. . . . Let us not withdraw our lips from this chalice prepared by the hand of Jesus. . . . Let us see life as it really is. . . . It is a moment, between two eternities. . . . Let us suffer in peace!. . . I admit that this word peace seemed a little strong to me, but the other day, when reflecting on it, I found the secret of suffering in peace. . . . The one who says peace is not saying joy, or at least felt joy. . . . To suffer in peace it is enough to will all that Jesus wills."

St. Therese of Lisieux
Love in the Heart of the Church

Thanksgiving

I will give thanks to you, O LORD, with all my heart,
   [for you have heard the words of my mouth];
   in the presence of the angels I will sing your
      praise;
I will worship at your holy temple
   and give thanks to your name,
Because of your kindness and your truth;
   for you have made great above all things
   your name and your promise.
When I called, you answered me;
   you built up strength within me.

Ps 138:1-3

Thanksgiving

O merciful and gracious Jesus, thank You for working wonders and bringing Your healing love to [name]. You sustained Your child through the illness, and blessed the recovery with Your Presence in Communion. Please prepare the way for Your friend's homecoming. May the angels accompany [name] and guard each footstep to keep [him, her] safe and in good health. O Sacrament Most Holy, O Sacrament Divine, all praise and all thanksgiving be every moment Thine!

First Communion Day. "It is impossible to describe what took place between my soul and Jesus. I asked Him a thousand times that He would take me and I experienced His Dear Voice for the first time. 'O Jesus I love You, I adore You!'. . . For the first time I felt a delicious peace. . . . That very happy day ended which will be the unique day of my life."

St. Teresa of the Andes
God the Joy of My Life

Alleluia.
Give thanks to the LORD, for he is good,
  for his mercy endures forever;
Give thanks to the God of gods,
  for his mercy endures forever;
Give thanks to the Lord of lords,
  for his mercy endures forever. . . .

Ps 136:1-3

Thanksgiving

O Eucharistic Heart of Jesus, we praise You and thank You for Your works! What more fitting way of thanking You could there be? Receiving You in Holy Communion is giving thanks. May the healing love You have poured out on [name] bring You glory. We thank You for the doctors and nurses who were instruments of Your healing love. Please bless them. Continue the healing You have begun in [name] as [he, she] returns home. May this renewed health proclaim Your mercy to all.

"O wealth of the poor, how admirably You know how to sustain souls! And without their seeing such great wealth, You show it to them little by little. When I behold majesty as extraordinary as this concealed in something as small as the Host, it happens afterward that I marvel at wisdom so wonderful, and I fail to know how the Lord gives me courage or strength to approach Him. If He who has granted, and still does grant me so many favors, did not give this strength, it would be impossible to conceal the fact or resist shouting aloud about marvels so great."

St. Teresa of Avila
Divine Intimacy, Vol. III

How to Pray

"This is how you are to pray:
  'Our Father in heaven,
  hallowed be your name,
  your kingdom come,
  your will be done
  on earth as it is in heaven.
  Give us today our daily bread,
  and forgive us the wrong we have done
  as we forgive those who wrong us.
  Subject us not to the trial
  but deliver us from the evil one.'"

Mt 6:9-13

How to Pray

O my Jesus, sometimes it is difficult to know how to pray. In our humanity we hope for miracles that heal, but Your wisdom sees far beyond the immediate desire. You know what is best. You tell us to pray for our daily bread, and Your friend confidently receives You, [his, her] Daily Bread. So I entrust [name] into Your loving Hands and pray: "Thy Will be done," knowing that Your will is perfect. In this total abandonment to Divine Providence is true peace.

"When His disciples asked Him to teach them to pray, Christ, obviously, as one Who knew so well His Father's will, would have told them all that was necessary in order to obtain an answer from the Eternal Father; and, in fact, He only taught them those seven petitions of the *Pater Noster*, which include all our spiritual and temporal necessities, and He did not teach numerous other kinds of prayers and ceremonies."

St. John of the Cross
Collected Works of St. John of the Cross

Liturgical Seasons

Go up onto a high mountain,
  Zion, herald of glad tidings;
Cry out at the top of your voice,
  Jerusalem, herald of good news!
Fear not to cry out
  and say to the cities of Judah:
  Here is your God!
Here comes with power
  the Lord GOD,
  who rules by his strong arm;
Here is his reward with him,
  his recompense before him.
Like a shepherd he feeds his flock;
  in his arms he gathers the lambs,
Carrying them in his bosom,
  and leading the ewes with care.

Is 40:9-11

Advent

Jesus, Your friend [name] makes this journey to Bethlehem in a hospital bed. It is a season of expectation and hope. As this dear one awaits the Great Day of Your Birth, may [he, she] remain with Our Lady and St. Joseph. May they show Your child how to prepare a loving welcome; and may the sufferings provide a warm bed to comfort You, Sweet Jesus. Draw Your dear one to Your stable and there bestow Your healing love.

"There is so much I still have to say to you about Christ, especially about His Incarnation for us in the Eucharist. The Word Incarnate is always there for us in the Eucharist. This overpowering mystery allows the unworthy hands of the priest to hold the same Body of Christ that the Virgin Mary held in her arms and pressed to her heart. Yet it is the same Christ! The priest takes Christ in his hands and gives Him to others!

When you receive Him, you are like the Virgin Mary during the months when she carried her Child. You truly carry Christ within you and want to be absorbed in profound thanksgiving. You carry Him living within you! How necessary is silence so that the Holy Spirit can reveal to us the grandeur of this mystery."

Fr. Jacques Bunel, OCD
Pere Jacques, Spiritual Guide

This day in David's city a savior has been born to you, the Messiah and Lord. Let this be a sign to you: in a manger you will find an infant wrapped in swaddling clothes. Suddenly, there was with the angel a multitude of the heavenly host, praising God and saying,

"Glory to God in high heaven,

peace on earth to those on whom his favor rests."

Lk 2:11-14

Christmas

O Sweet Infant of Bethlehem, You have come as Infant King and Sacred Host to spend Your holy Feast with [name]. How much love Your presence brings! You are pure Gift. May You gaze on Your friend with Your radiant Face and clutch [him, her] in Your little Hand. May Your smile ravish, heal and cause [name's] heart to leap for joy!

"To be a child of God means: to be led by the Hand of God, to do the Will of God, not one's own will, to place every care and hope into the Hand of God and not to worry about oneself or the future. On this rests the freedom and the joy of the child of God."

St. Edith Stein
Reflections

[T]herefore he had to become like his brothers in every way, that he might be a merciful and faithful high priest before God on their behalf, to expiate the sins of the people. Since he was himself tested through what he suffered, he is able to help those who are tempted.

Heb 2:17, 18

Lent

Jesus in this Holy Season, You have invited Your friend to share Your Cross. You have called [name] away from normal activity into the desert as You have done. In this illness Your friend also experiences testing as You did. Let these days be spent in prayer and offering of all the sufferings that each day brings. May Your child run to embrace the Cross You so lovingly offer, and through it be brought to healing Resurrection joy!

"The star of Bethlehem shines in the night of sin. The shadow of the Cross falls on the light that shines from the Crib. The light is extinguished in the darkness of Good Friday, but it rises all the more brilliantly as the sun of grace on the morning of the Resurrection. The way of the incarnate Son of God leads through the Cross and Passion to the glory of the Resurrection. In His company the way of every one of us, indeed of all mankind, leads through suffering and death to this same glorious goal."

St. Edith Stein
Reflections

Yet it was our infirmities that he bore,
   our sufferings that he endured,
While we thought of him as stricken,
   as one smitten by God and afflicted.
But he was pierced for our offenses,
   crushed for our sins,
Upon him was the chastisement that makes us
     whole,
   by his stripes we were healed.

                    Is 53:4, 5

Lent

Sweet Jesus, You loved us all the way to Calvary. Your body was not spared any horror or indignity. You understand the trials of Your suffering people. In this season of Lent You have called [name] to share Your sufferings. As Your friend clings to You on the Cross, let drops of Your Precious Blood fall on [him, her] to bring healing. Send angels to comfort Your chosen one as they comforted You in the Garden. On Easter may [name] also share the joy of the Resurrection in good health.

"There is no need or trial or persecution that is not easy to suffer if we begin to enjoy the delight and consolation of this Sacred Bread."

St. Teresa of Avila
Collected Works of St. Teresa of Avila, Vol. II

Meanwhile, Mary stood weeping beside the tomb. Even as she wept, she stooped to peer inside, and there she saw two angels in dazzling robes. One was seated at the head and the other at the foot of the place where Jesus' body had lain. "Woman," they asked her, "why are you weeping?" She answered them, "Because the Lord has been taken away, and I do not know where they have put him."

She had no sooner said this than she turned around and caught sight of Jesus standing there. But she did not know him. "Woman," he asked her, "why are you weeping? Who is it you are looking for?" She supposed he was the gardener, so she said, "Sir, if you are the one who carried him off, tell me where you have laid him and I will take him away." Jesus said to her, "Mary!" She turned to him and said [in Hebrew], "Rabbouni!"(meaning "Teacher").

Jn 20:11-16

Easter

O Risen Jesus, You bring hope to the world, and new light where there is darkness. Just as You appeared to Mary in the garden, You now come to be with [name]. Jesus, Our Eucharistic Love, we thank You for what You have done for us. Your Resurrection gives cause for joy even where there is sickness and suffering. As Your dear one celebrates Your Holy Resurrection, may You touch and heal [him, her].

"At 5:00 AM we have the Mass of the Resurrection followed by a magnificent procession in our beautiful garden. Everything was so still, so mysterious, that it seemed our Master was going to appear to us along the solitary paths as He once appeared to Mary Magdalene. And if our eyes did not see Him, at least our souls met Him in faith."

Bl. Elizabeth of the Trinity
Light Love Life

When the day of Pentecost came it found them gathered in one place. Suddenly from up in the sky there came a noise like a strong, driving wind which was heard all through the house where they were seated. Tongues as of fire appeared, which parted and came to rest on each of them. All were filled with the Holy Spirit. They began to express themselves in foreign tongues and make bold proclamation as the Spirit prompted them.

Acts 2:1-4

Pentecost

O Holy Spirit, Beloved of our souls, You have come with the Father and the Son to be with [name]. O Heavenly Fire, on this Feast may the flames of Your Love bring healing and wholeness where there is sickness and suffering. May You console and strengthen [name] that [he, she] may proclaim Your marvelous deeds!

"He [Jesus] handed us the wine so that, drinking it, we might lead his life, might share his suffering. Whoever wishes to do my will, let him daily take up his cross. . . . And when his disciples did not understand that his way would be a way of suffering, he explained this to them and said, 'Should not the Christ so suffer, in order to enter into his glory?'

"Then the hearts of the disciples burned within them. God's word had set them on fire. And when the Holy Spirit had descended on them to fan that divine fire into flame, then they were glad to suffer scorn and persecution, whereby they resembled him who had preceded them on the way of suffering."

Bl. Titus Brandsma, OCD
Carmelite Proper of the Liturgy of the Hours

"This is the bread that came down from heaven.
Unlike your ancestors who ate and died nonethe-
less,
the man who feeds on this bread shall live forever."

Jn 6:58

Corpus Christi

O True Body and Blood of Jesus we greet You on Your Sacred Feast with hearts that are hungry and yearning for You. Jesus, Healer of the sick, Beloved of our hearts, You have come to [name] who is sick. You are at the same time Doctor and Medicine, Sacrifice and Priest. Please hear [name's] prayers; and by the greatness of Your Love in this Holy Sacrament bestow Your healing.

"Receiving the Holy Sacraments that draw strength from Your Blood and from Your passion, we come by their means to taste the sweetness of the passion, and of the Blood that was shed therein. We savor this most fully when we receive the Holy Sacrament of Your Body and Blood, for there more than anywhere else this sweetness and grace are found hidden, when the Sacrament is really received with purity and honesty. Let whoever wishes to taste of Your gentleness and sweetness approach this Blood and there he will find all rest and consolation."

St. Mary Magdalen de' Pazzi
Divine Intimacy, Vol. III

For thus says the Lord GOD: I myself will look after and tend my sheep. As a shepherd tends his flock when he finds himself among his scattered sheep, so will I tend my sheep. I will rescue them from every place where they were scattered when it was cloudy and dark. . . . I myself will pasture my sheep; I myself will give them rest, says the Lord GOD. The lost I will seek out, the strayed I will bring back, the injured I will bind up, the sick I will heal [but the sleek and the strong I will destroy], shepherding them rightly.

Ez 34:11, 12, 15-17

Christie the King

O Jesus, Our Eucharistic King, You do not remain aloof from Your people, Your creatures. In order to be approachable by all of Your people You hide Your Magnificence in this little Host. You come with Your healing love to restore and refresh Your suffering friends. You call [name] and invite [him, her] to dine with You and to share in Your Kingdom. Please bless and heal and restore Your little one as You come to stay. You are truly the King of Kings!

"How meek and humble of heart Thou dost appear, my beloved Saviour, when I look upon Thee hidden under the white Host! Thou couldst not stoop lower in order to teach me humility. I, therefore, in return for Thy love will put myself in the last place and share Thy humiliations, that I may have a part with Thee in the kingdom of Heaven. I beg of Thee to send me a humiliation every time I try to exalt myself above others."

St. Therese of Lisieux
Just For Today

Bibliography

Benedictine of Stanbrook. *Just For Today*. Springfield, IL: Templegate Publishers, 1988.

Brunot, Amedee, scj. *Mariam: "The Little Arab."* Eugene, OR: The Carmel of Maria Regina, 1990.

Carrouges, Michael. *Pere Jacques, Spiritual Guide*. New York, NY: The Macmillan Company, 1961.

Centala, Theodore, ocd. *Carmel Clarion*, Washington, D.C: Carmelite Friary, 1998, February/March 1998.

Clarke, John, ocd. *Story of a Soul*. Washington, D.C: ICS, 1976.

De La Vierge, R.P. Victor, ocd. *Spiritual Realism of St. Therese of Lisieux*. Milwaukee, WI: Bruce Publishing Company, 1961.

De Meester, Conrad, ocd. *Light Love Life: Elizabeth of the Trinity*. Washington, D.C: ICS, 1987.

Gabriel of St. Mary Magdalen, Fr. *Divine Intimacy, Vol. III*. San Francisco, CA: Ignatius Press, 1987.

Gabriel of St. Mary Magdalen, Fr. *Divine Intimacy, Vol. IV*. San Francisco, CA: Ignatius Press, 1987.

Griffin, Michael, OCD, trans. *God the Joy of My Life*. Washington, D.C.: Teresian Charism Press, 1989.

Griffin, Michael, OCD, trans. *Letters of St. Teresa of the Andes*. Hubertus, WI: Teresian Charism Press, 1994.

Griffin, Michael, OCD, trans. *Lingering with My Lord*. New York, NY: Alba House, 1985.

Lawrence of the Resurrection, OCD. *The Practice of the Presence of God*. Old Tappan, NJ: Fleming H. Revell Company, 1967.

O'Donnell, Christopher, O.CARM. *Love in the Heart of the Church*. Dublin: Veritas Publications, 1997.

Rodriguez, Otilio, OCD, trans., and Kavanaugh, Kieran, OCD, trans. *The Collected Works of St. John of the Cross*. Washington, D.C: ICS, 1979.

Rodriguez, Otilio, OCD, trans., and Kavanaugh, Kieran, OCD, trans. *The Collected Works of St. Teresa of Avila, Vol. II*. Washington, D.C: ICS, 1980.

Rogge, Louis, O.CARM. *Proper of the Liturgy of the Hours of the Order of the Brothers of the Blessed Virgin Mary of Mt. Carmel and of the Order of Discalced Carmelites*. Rome: Institutum Carmelitanum, 1993.

Stein, Edith (Teresa Benedicta of the Cross, OCD). *Reflections*. Darlington: Carmel of Darlington, 1982.

Stein, Edith (Teresa Benedicta of the Cross, OCD). *Self Portrait in Letters*. Washington, D.C: ICS, 1993.